NCT #127
Neo Zone : The Final Round
TAEIL, JOHNNY, TAEYONG, YUTA, DOYOUNG,
JAEHYUN, JUNGWOO, MARK, HAECHAN.

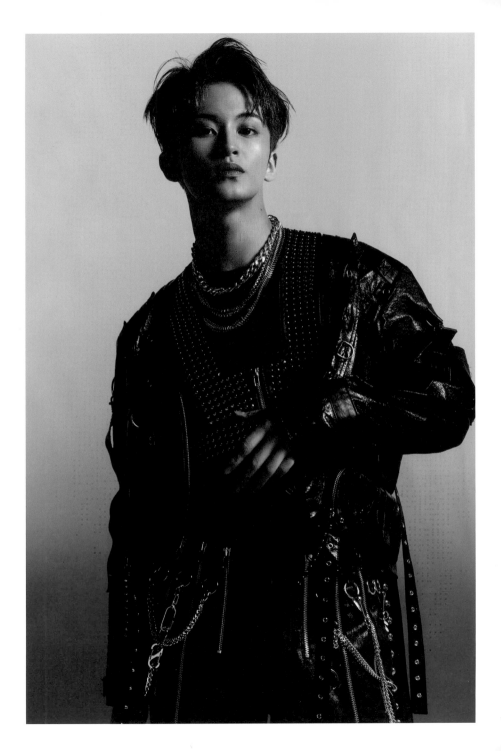

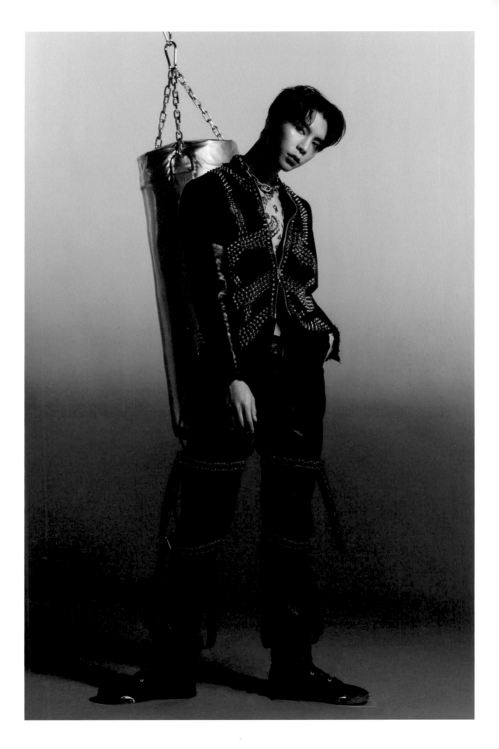

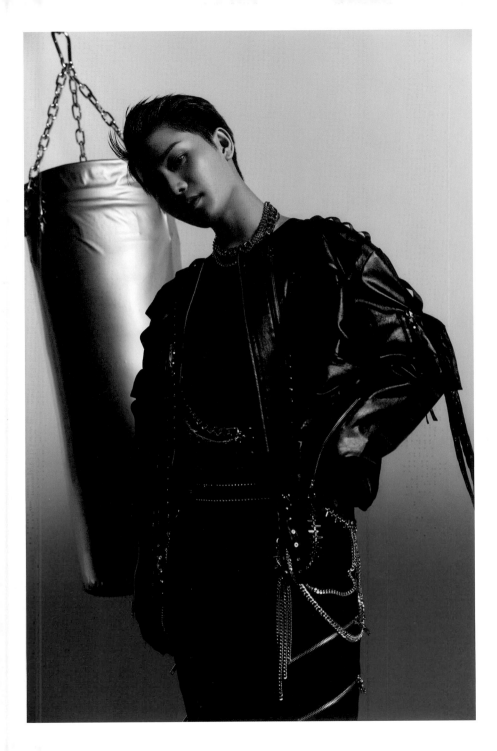

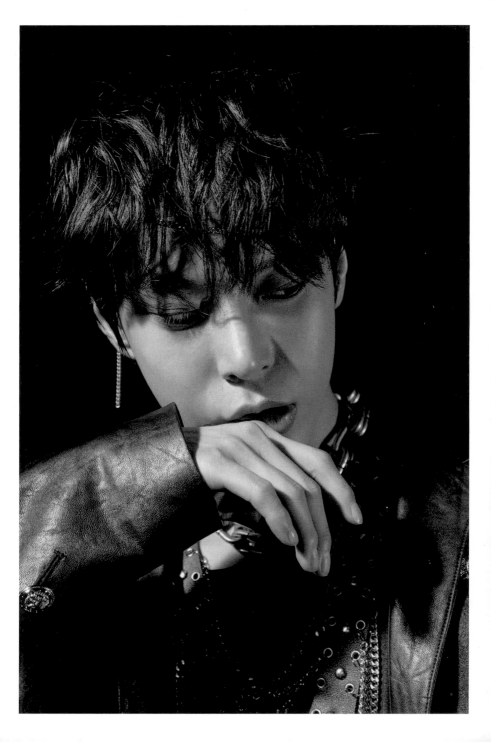

punch

||||||||||||||||||||||||||||||||||

Korean Lyrics by
Kenzie

Composed by
Kenzie / Dwayne "Dem
Jointz" Abernathy Jr. /
Keynon "KC" Moore

Arranged by
Kenzie / Dwayne "Dem
Jointz" Abernathy Jr. /
Alawn / 라이언 전

한 방 Puncher 다 휘청거려 해머 아웃 날려 'cause I'm a clean fighter / 뭘 망설여 네 셔틀은 느려 더 바짝 붙어 언제 깰래 wake up! / gong이 울려 함성도 커져 내 피가 끓어 거칠게 없어 / we the future and we are dreamerz / 링은 뒤집히고 우린 꽤 제법 하지

Hot hot hot / 자 더블 타임 스윙 내 귓속의 gig 그 비트 위로 힛 / 찢겨진 데시벨 on the 32nd beat / 한계 없는 gain my mix straight bang like

Hot hot hot 또 lick을 쏟아대 / styles make a fight 거짓말 안 해 / As high as we can get As loud as we can get / 준비한 자가 차지해 we got the championship

거칠었던 라운드 난 다음을 준비해 / 메말랐던 너의 영혼 적셔 줄 나이기에 / 매 순간 처음인 듯 일어날 나이길

*Hey We Ballin' / We fight together / That punch! 날리고 / 더 뛰고 소리쳐 Babe / 가슴은 뜨거워 yeah yeah / Hey We Ballin' / 전부를 바꿀 파이터 / 내 세상으로 와 / 우리가 누구야 babe hey we ballin'

혼자만의 소우주 그 안의 긴 긴 싸움 달리고 또 달려도 멀어 보인 그 출구 / 너의 신호 느꼈지 나만의 빛을 본거지 풀려지는 그 비밀 너만이 나의 exit

Ha ha ha 쏟아진 환희 난 숨 몰아쉬어 눈 똑바로 떠 / As high as we can get As loud as we can get / 대세는 정해져 우리가 다 날려 Punch!

거칠었던 라운드 난 다음을 준비해 / 매 순간 처음인 듯 일어날 나이길

Hey We Ballin' / We fight together / That punch! 날리고

이 빛 아래 꿈꾸는 듯해 / 뜨거움이 멈추지 않기를 더 원해 one more time one more time / 큰 세계로 끝없이 달려가 후회 없이 난 싸워볼래 my show goes on

*Repeat

Hey We Ballin'

Vocal Directed by Kenzie Background Vocals by NCT 도영 / NCT 태일 / NCT 해찬 / NCT 재현 / NCT 정우 Recorded by 노민지 @ SM Yellow Tail Studio Digital Editing by 정유라 / 노민지 @ SM Yellow Tail Studio Engineered for Mix by 노민지 @ SM Yellow Tail Studio Mixed by 정의석 @ SM Blue Cup Studio

Original Title: Whatchamacall Us   Original Writers: Kenzie / Dwayne "Dem Jointz" Abernathy Jr. / Keynon "KC" Moore / Harold "Alawn" Philippon / 라이언 전   Original Publishers: EKKO Music Rights (powered by CTGA) / Dem Jointz Music / BMG Platinum Songs US / Musikade / Marcan Entertainment Sub-Publishers: Fujipacific Music Korea Inc. / Musikade

nonstop

yeh yeh yeh yeh yeh

넌 끊임없이 flow futuristic and I 주윌 맴도는 밤 / 미친 속도 뒤집혀진 lanes at a hundread and five / 네가 원하는 건 많아 어쨌건 난 답을 알아 더욱 가까워진 찰나 all time

순간들이 있어 무너져 버릴 뻔한 / 너를 안았을까 그 때 멈춰 서 버렸다면 / never messin' up the flow

넌 위험하고 날 뒤흔들어 / 감당 못할 이상향으로 / 이 절망과 환희조차 다 너를 위한 거라고

*I want it nonstop I want it I won't drop for nothing 시간도 공간도 운명까지 / 세상 끝에 무지비한 벽에 부딪혀 넘어져 머무르지 않게 / 기다려 늦지 않아 달려가 너를 안을 테니까 / NonStop 멈추지 않아 wanna ride 네게 달려가

이름조차 없던 세상을 겉돌던 방황들 다 끝나 이제 마주할 영원 / keep rollin' call my name like no slowin' / you're where I'm supposed to be / no stallin' need that need that big ballin'

긴 숨을 쉬곤 해 멈추지 않기 위해 / 잠시 비틀거렸지만 이젠 더 흔들리지 않아 / never messin' up the flow

바라만 보고 널 갈구하고 / 포기 못할 이유를 준 너 / 이 절망과 환희조차 다 너를 위한 거라고

*Repeat

can't stop won't stop / I can't stop nonstop ya

밤의 태양도 원한다면 찾을게 (can't stop won't stop) / 어디든 네가 찾는 그 사람 될게 (I can't stop nonstop ya) / 세상 끝 어디라도 날 불러줘

*Repeat

how we doin' / ah yeah ah yeah ya! ya! / can't stop nonstop / can't stop nonstop ya

Korean Lyrics by Kenzie

Composed by Kenzie / Greg Bonnick / Hayden Chapman / Adrian Mckinnon

Arranged by LDN Noise

Vocal Directed by Kenzie Background Vocals by NCT 도영 / NCT 태일 / NCT 해찬 / NCT 재현 / Kenzie / Adrian Mckinnon Recorded by 정의석 @ SM Blue Cup Studio Digital Editing by 이지홍 @ SM LVYIN Studio Engineered for Mix by 이지홍 @ SM LVYIN Studio Mixed by 김한구 @ sound POOL studios

Original Title: NonStop Original Writers: Kenzie / Greg Bonnick / Hayden Chapman / Adrian Mckinnon Original Publishers: EKKO Music Rights (powered by CTGA) / AMM 7 / WC Music Corp. Sub-Publisher: Warner Chappell Music Korea Inc.

Composed by
DEEZ / Dwayne "Dem
Jointz" Abernathy Jr. /
YOO, YOUNG JIN

Arranged by
DEEZ

Mixed by 김철순 @ SM Blue Ocean Studio

Original Title: 서곡 (序曲; Prelude) Original Writer: DEEZ Production Administered by Dwayne "Dem Jointz" Abernathy Jr. / YOO, YOUNG JIN Original Publishers: EKKO Music Rights (powered by CTGA) / Dem Jointz Music / BMG Platinum Songs US Sub-Publisher: Fujipacific Music Korea Inc.

영웅 [英雄; Kick It]

Let me introduce you to some new thangs new thangs new thangs / bass kick swingin' like I'm Bruce Lee Bruce Lee Bruce Lee / shimmy shimmy shimmy 불이 붙네 불이 붙네 이 무대 위로 뜰 때 / 난 앞으로 찔러 좌우 Bruce Lee 날아다녀 하루 종일 Bruce Lee

comin' up 지금 여기로 baby 이 느낌은 이해 못 해 머리론 / fighting for all day 아무 생각 말고 너의 이야기대로 걸어

어두운 어제가 오늘을 삼켜버리기 전에 / 내 목소린 더 퍼져야 해 소리치면 돼 / 내겐 no more trauma

baby we go wild / one two seven squad / 난 앞으로 질러 pow / 좌우로 내질러 pow

난 앞으로 찔러 좌우 new thangs new thangs new thangs / 우리가 어딜 가든 축제 들어 축배 like my birthday / 모두 감아 차올리지 높이 where ma roof at 지붕이 우주에 (na na na na na na) / 난 앞으로 찔러 좌우 Bruce Lee 날아다녀 하루 종일 Bruce Lee (na na na na na na)

(Ya!) I got that drip 흘러넘쳐 Guts 잃어버린 겁 / 어디서든 make it poppin' keep it movin' like 'Jeet Kune' / 내 앞을 막을 땐 'Samuel Jackson' 돼 wassup? / 배배 꼬인 놈 baby you just gotta watch

'Enter The Dragon' 난 영화같이 / 걸음걸이마저 Martial Arts / looking that everybody looking at me / Cams Action Movie shh / 쓰러뜨려 하나씩 / (쉿!) blows away 자비는 없지 ruthless / droppin' the bomb on ma enemies / and I'm gonna kick it like Bruce Lee

수많은 날들의 같은 장면을 반복한 끝에 / 어제의 날 무너뜨리고 소리치면 돼 / 내겐 no more trauma

baby we go wild / one two seven squad / we ain't never gonna stop / 끝이 안 보여도 가

난 앞으로 찔러 좌우 new thangs new thangs new thangs (na na na na na na) / 난 앞으로 찔러 좌우 Bruce Lee 날아다녀 하루 종일 Bruce Lee (na na na na na na)

my world 만들어가 yeah / 상상조차 할 수 없었던 아주 극적인 장면 그 깊은 곳에 / 눈앞에 펼쳐질 새로운 세상들 손안에 잡힐 듯 내 안으로 들어와 / 어둠 끝에 다시 난 새로 태어나

난 앞으로 찔러 좌우 new thangs new thangs new thangs / 우리가 어딜 가든 축제 들어 축배 like my birthday (eh eh eh eh eh eh)

shimmy shimmy shimmy 불이 훅 shimmy shimmy shimmy 훅 / 높이 where ma roof at 지붕이 우주에 (na na na na na na) / 난 앞으로 찔러 좌우 Bruce Lee 날아다녀 하루 종일 Bruce Lee (na na na na na na) / 날아다녀 하루 종일 Bruce Lee

Korean Lyrics by
우탄 / Rick Bridges (X&) /
danke (lalala studio)

Composed by
Dwayne "Dem Jointz"
Abernathy Jr. /
Mayila Jones / Rodnae
"Chikk" Bell / DEEZ /
YOO, YOUNG JIN / 라이언 전

Arranged by
Dwayne "Dem Jointz"
Abernathy Jr. / DEEZ /
YOO, YOUNG JIN

Vocal Directed by DEEZ / YOO, YOUNG JIN Background Vocals by YOO, YOUNG JIN / NCT 도영 / NCT 해찬 / NCT 태일 Recorded by YOO, YOUNG JIN @ SM BOOMINGSYSTEM / 김광민 @ 개니리싸운드 Digital Editing by YOO, YOUNG JIN @ SM BOOMINGSYSTEM / 장우영 @ doobdoob Studio / 이지홍 @ SM LVYIN Studio Engineered for Mix by YOO, YOUNG JIN @ SM BOOMINGSYSTEM / 이지홍 @ SM LVYIN Studio Mixed by 김철순 @ SM Blue Ocean Studio

Original Title: Bruce Lee Original Writers: Dwayne "Dem Jointz" Abernathy Jr. / Mayila Jones / Rodnae "Chikk" Bell / DEEZ / YOO, YOUNG JIN / 라이언 전 Original Publishers: Dem Jointz Music / BMG Platinum Songs US / Jones Music / Se'Lah Publishing / EKKO Music Rights (powered by CTGA) / Marcan Entertainment Sub-Publishers: Fujipacific Music Korea Inc. / Musikade

꿈 (Boom)

||||||||||||||||||||||||||||||||||||||

Korean Lyrics by
서지음

Composed by
Kevin White / Mike Woods /
Andrew Bazzi / MZMC

Arranged by
Rice N' Peas

하나 둘 셋 넷 / 꿈속의 꿈일까 깨도 똑같아 / 아침부터 저녁까지 깊고 긴 꿈에 빠진 느낌 / 부풀어 내 맘이 하루에도 몇 번씩 / Lose it all for a night with you / trade in anything make my dreams come true

왠지 좋았어 baby 그림처럼 다시 네가 거기 서있던 날 / 스친 그날 이후로 모든 순간들이 너에게로 스며들어

*난 요즘 everyday aye / 널 떠올리기 전부터 널 떠올리곤 해 / 그때마다 yeah aye / 웃는 것도 모른 채로 웃고 있곤 해 yeah

**Can you take all my love? 널 그려 난 지금 / 다시 떠올라 내 맘이 이번에는 좀 더 멀리 / 내게만 열리는 꿈보다 꿈같은 / 구름보다 높은 곳을 혼자 떠다니는 나

***Boom

난 여기 혼자 멈춰버려도 좋아 아직 깨고 싶지 않아 no no / 이건 나의 노래 서툰 고백 들린다면 받아줘 oh

*Repeat

**Repeat

***Repeat

sunlight or moonlight 그 무엇을 비춰도 아름다워 / 난 시간이 멈춘 채 너의 먼 대답만을 기다려 / 난 긴장한 채로 긴 신호음에 맞춰 / 네 맘을 두드리고 있어 ooh 내가 들리니

수화기 너머로 들리는 작은 숨 / 다시 떠올라 내 맘이 / 이번에는 좀 더 멀리 / 어쩌면 넌 지금 나와 같은 생각 중일까 / 이 모든 게 멈춰진 순간

***Repeat

***Repeat

Vocal Directed by 주찬양 (ICONIC SOUNDS) **Background Vocals by** 주찬양 (ICONIC SOUNDS) **Recorded by** 장우영, 권유진, 민성수 @ doobdoob Studio **Digital Editing by** 노민지 @ SM SSAM Studio **Engineered for Mix by** 이민규 @ SM Big Shot Studio / 노민지 @ SM SSAM Studio **Mixed by** 김철순 @ SM Blue Ocean Studio

Original Title: Boom Original Writers: Mike Woods / Kevin White / Andrew Bazzi / MZMC Original Publisher: MZMC Inc Korea Co., Ltd.

낮잠 (pandora's box)

간지러운 숨소리에 웃음이 나 잠들어 있는 표정까지 좋으니까 / 날 감싸는 오후의 부드러운 햇살에 안긴 채로 작은 꿈을 꿔

이 순간에 난 너만을 담아 너만을 담아 내 마음에 가득히 새기고 / 어느샌가 난 두 눈을 감아 네게로 love love love

*귓가에 너의 숨결이 자장가처럼 닿을 때 / 달콤한 넌 pandora's box oh 달콤한 넌 / 나른한 오후 햇살이 내 맘에 스며들 때면 / 빠져드는 pandora's box pandora's box pandora's box

내 어깨를 어루만진 햇살이 포근해서 잠이 들어 너처럼 / 같은 꿈을 꿀 것만 같아서

따뜻하게 내 온몸을 감싸와 어제와 오늘 그리고 내일 / 너와 날 가득 채워가

이 순간에 난 너만을 담아 너만을 담아 내 마음에 가득히 널 새기고 / 어느샌가 난 두 눈을 감아 네게로 love love love

*Repeat

**기억해 이 순간의 우리 우리를 / 언제나 이렇게 together forever / 기억해 이 순간의 우리 우리를 / 언제나 이렇게 together forever

알잖아 baby 언제나 ride or die with you 어디든 좋아 함께라면 paradise everyday / 편안한 이 바람 smooth 마치 가까운 너의 숨처럼 느껴지는 이 순간 눈을 감고 간직해

낮에 보는 꿈 빠져들어 hole 필요 없이 tool / 너는 나의 베개 나는 너의 이불이 되어주곤 하고 but / 피곤하긴 해 두근댈 때에 심장이 자꾸 너란 숨결에 닿아서 오늘도 포근해

good times these nights / your eyes a different scene / breathes so close we see / you take mine away from me

매일 넌 나를 꿈꾸게 해 / 거짓말 같은 꿈속에 yeah

함께할 모든 순간이 소중한 너란 기적이 / 날 기다린 pandora's box oh pandora's box / 내 꿈에 담긴 기억이너라는 모든 시간이 / 우리만의 pandora's box pandora's box pandora's box

**Repeat

Korean Lyrics by
JQ / 현지원 (makeumine works) / 김혜지 (makeumine works) / 태용 / 마크 / 쟈니

Composed by
Erik Lidbom

Arranged by
Erik Lidbom for Hitfire Production

Vocal Directed by 전승우 Background Vocals by 전승우 Recorded by 장우영, 민성수, 권유진 @ doobdoob Studio Digital Editing by 노민지 @ SM SSAM Studio Engineered for Mix by 노민지 @ SM SSAM Studio Mixed by 남궁진 @ SM Concert Hall Studio

Original Title: Pandora's Box Original Writer: Erik Lidbom Original Publisher: Hitfire Publishing Sub-Publisher: Music Cube, Inc.

Day Dream (白日夢)

Korean Lyrics by
황유빈

Composed by
Ian Jeffrey Thomas /
Hannah Wilson / Ariowa
Irosogie / Andrew Beckner

Arranged by
Ian Jeffrey Thomas

어디쯤 이런 바람이 불어온 건지 자꾸만 나를 한 걸음씩 떠밀어 어지러 / 수풀 사잇길 헤매는데 마침 익숙히 스친 멜로디 / na na na na na na

고갤 돌린 순간 날 불러낸 듯한 / oh you oh my 난 빠져들어가 for love

*Loving you feels like I'm dreaming 난 별 따라 / 어디까지 온 걸까 no / Loving you feels like I'm dreaming 넌 날 알아 / 너의 이름이 뭐야? no huh

신세계 같아 여기는 oh my my my 둘러보기도 바빠 not tired tired tired / 순간 어디선가 몰래 나타나 미소만 남긴 cheshire cat

이 모두를 내게만 다 열어 준 듯한 / oh you and I 더 빠져들어가 for love

*Repeat

걸음이 아주 빨라 저만치 나를 앞서 그럼 눈을 감어 그렇게 너를 찾아 / 쏟아낸 질문 그저 티 없이 넌 미소 지을 뿐 다시 한번 되물었어 no / 너의 이름이 뭐냐고 / my cherry blossom / it ain't fall yet so don't leave / we can solve it (we can solve it)

Loving you feels like I'm dreaming 꿈만 같아 / 깨어나고 싶지 않아 no / Loving you feels like I'm dreaming 숨이 가빠 / 헤어나고 싶지 않아 no

Vocal Directed by 서미래 (ButterFly) Background Vocals by NCT 도영 / 서미래 (ButterFly) / Ariowa Irosogie Recorded by 이지홍, 노민지 @ Yellow Tail Studio / 권유진, 민성수 @ doobdoob Studio Pro Tools Operating by 서미래 (ButterFly) Digital Editing by 서미래 (ButterFly) / 노민지 @ SM SSAM Studio Engineered for Mix by 노민지 @ SM SSAM Studio Mixed by 구종필 @ KLANG STUDIO

Original Title: Dreamin Original Writers: Ariowa Irosogie / Hannah Wilson / Ian Jeffrey Thomas / Andrew Beckner Original Publishers: Warner Chappell Music Ltd / Phrased Differently Music Limited / Music By ITC Publishing / Songs of Atlas Music Group / Copyright Control Sub-Publishers: Warner Chappell Music Korea Inc. / Fujipacific Music Korea Inc.

너의 하루 (Make Your Day)

어느 날 다음날도 다시 이어진 다음날도 / 믿어지지가 않아 나의 모든 순간 이렇게 eh / 너와 함께할 수 있단 게

ooh 하얀 커튼 너머에 저 햇살마저 파도처럼 밀려와 this is your day / 또 너로 인해 내 오늘마저 기적이 된 걸 혹시 너는 알까

*일 년에 단 하루만으론 한없이 모자란 걸 / 매일 아침 눈뜨는 너를 향해 oh / 속삭여 줄래 오늘 행복하길 바랄게

ooh 그냥 너라는 존재 그것만으로 이렇게나 빛이 나 눈부시게 / oh nah 널 만난 후에 날 둘러싸던 이 모든 게 다 꿈인 것만 같아

*Repeat

난 스며들고 싶어 너의 곁에 uh / 그 언제라도 늘 네 편이 될게 my dear / 매일 너와 함께 할게 / 날마다 영원히

oh your birthday / 일 년에 그 하루 말고도 다 너의 날이었으면 / 매일 아침 눈 뜨는 널 향해 / 너의 하루 오늘 행복하길 바랄게

너의 모든 날을 축하해

Korean Lyrics by
서지음

Composed by
Andrew Choi /
밍지션 (minGtion)

Arranged by
밍지션 (minGtion)

Vocal Directed by 밍지션 (minGtion) Background Vocals by NCT 도영 / Andrew Choi Bass Performed by 밍지션 (minGtion) Guitar Performed by 박신원 Piano Performed by 밍지션 (minGtion) Strings Performed by 융스트링 Strings Arranged by 한성은 Recorded by 이지홍, 강은지 @ SM LVYIN Studio / 정기홍 (assist. 최다인, 이진미) @ Seoul Studio Digital Editing by 밍지션 (minGtion) Engineered for Mix by 노민지 @ SM Yellow Tail Studio Mixed by 남궁진 @ SM Concert Hall Studio

Original Title: Who I Am Original Writers: Andrew Choi / 밍지션 (minGtion) Original Publisher: EKKO Music Rights (powered by CTGA)

Composed & Arranged by
SQUAR (BLUR)

Narration by
지니

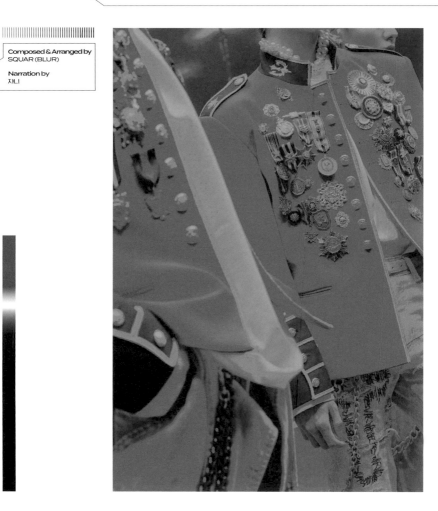

Recorded by 이민규 @ SM Big Shot Studio **Mixed by** 이민규 @ SM Big Shot Studio

Original Title: Interlude: Neo Zone Original Writer: SQUAR (BLUR) Original Publisher: X&

뿔 (MAD DOG)

Jumping on my trauma / already wear pajamas / 편안함을 유지해
너는 감당 못해 NADA / 내 마음속 안에 뿔이 자라나야 어딜 봐어서 빨리 달아나

drop it let it go pop it let it show / 심장에 붙은 뿔은 불이 나지 let it blow /
다시 drop it let it go pop it let it show / 건드리면 터져 난 진짜 MAD
DOG (whoa)

*지금까진 teaser 기대해 MAD DOG (whoa) / 건드리면 터져 난 진짜 MAD
DOG (whoa) / 자 이제 튀어 자 뛰어 MAD DOG (whoa) / 건드리면 터져 난
진짜 MAD DOG (whoa)

hunt or be hunted / 멱살 허전해 / 2 3개 이어 100 only sky's the limit /
발목 잡히는 일 없게 all day 날아다녀 okay / 엄한 대로 엄격하게 we go hard
불질러 mayday

drop it let it go pop it let it show / 지금 속도라면 아마 끝엔 싹 다 gone /
I said drop it let it go pop it let it show / we blow with the bass
drop it's time for MAD DOG

*Repeat

어둠 속에 흔들리는 붉은빛이 / welcome to the party / 회색 도시 그림자를
물들이고 / welcome to my nightmare

what's that on your mind feeling alienated / Imma tear opinions
down 나는 네 꿈속 에일리언 / 네 마음 깊은 곳 뿔이 자라나 / we making a
new world come in with me

hold on yeah you know us / you know we run the scene / yeah
예의 갖춰 꾸벅 선명해지는 screen / 외쳐 'Mea culpa' 이윽고 내가 뚜벅 /
yeah this is how we do it no flex keep it moving

drop it let it go pop it let it show / 1분 1초가 아까워 지금 아님 뭐 / 다시
drop it let it go pop it let it show / 건드리면 터져 난 진짜 MAD DOG
(whoa)

*Repeat

no flex yeah uh huh / I'm about to blow

건드리면 터져 난 진짜 MAD DOG (whoa)

Korean Lyrics by
김부민 / 태용 / 마크

Composed by
Hitchhiker / Charles
Stephens / John Fulford
/ Christopher Newland

Arranged by
Hitchhiker

Vocal Directed by Hitchhiker, 김부민 Guitar and Keyboards performed by Hitchhiker Recorded by 홍수연 @ 게나리싸운드 Digital Editing by
Hitchhiker / 이민규 @ SM Big Shot Studio Engineered for Mix by 이민규 @ SM Big Shot Studio Mixed by 이민규 @ SM Big Shot Studio

Original Title: Made of Dough Original Writers: Hitchhiker / Charles Stephens / John Fulford / Christopher Newland / 김부민 Original
Publishers: EKKO Music Rights (powered by CTGA) / CS 3RD Music Publishing Administered by Spirit Two Music (ASCAP) /
Entertainment Asset Partners (ASCAP) / Copyright Control (BMI) Sub-Publisher: MACO n MAJOR Entertainment, Inc.

sit Down!

Korean Lyrics by
황유빈! / Tommy $trate

Composed by
Harvey Mason Jr. /
Kevin Randolph /
Dewain Whitmore /
Patrick "J Que" Smith /
Britt Burton

Arranged by
Harvey Mason Jr. /
Kevin Randolph

ya ok ya!

I got a bad habit 문제가 많지 난 / 정답은 싹 지워 내 답은 내가 쓰지 / 네가 왜 내 발을 묶어? I'll be a pilot / 날아저 space까지 내 삶을 조종해 fly

It's a cruel game I cannot lose / 이 길 위에 movin' like we on a cruise / always maintain / 차분함을 지켜야해 so groove ooh

흔들릴 땐 조금 더 먼 곳을 봐 / 한 눈엔 다 담지 못할 꿈을 그려봐 / baby babe uh 눈을 뜬 그 순간

*(ay you ay you) Sit down! (don't tell me what to be) Sit down! (don't tell me where to be) Sit down! (I'll show u how to be) Sit down! / zip it lock it down

don't get up don't stand up / please don't put your hand up / and don't make me tell you again / Sit down!

눈이 내 말보다 더 강력해 난 말을 아껴 관심 없을 때 / 나서지 마 잘 생각해 너답게 하면 돼 It's your day

넌 꿈을 배워 like nonsense 왜 점수를 매겨 난 no thanks / 난 통제를 넘어 정상에 서 다 정상이 아냐 renegade

I smell some jealousy (I smell some jealousy) / you should just let that be (let it go) / 누가 뭐라 하든 그냥 걸어 갈래 my way / 내가 찾던 heaven 거길 데려가줄 highway

흔들릴 땐 여기 내 옆에 기대 / 뺏기지 못할 그 꿈을 더 키워가 봐 / baby babe oh 이제 손을 뻗어

*Repeat

세상의 크기에 널 맞추려 하지 마 수없이 부딪칠 수는 있지만 / 깨지고 부서져 작은 한 조각이 될 순 없잖아 / 결국에 너와 난 같은 꿈속에서 yeah we all know / 큰 꿈을 그려 yeah yeah / 세상의 퍼즐이 모두 맞춰지도록

*Repeat

*Repeat

Sit down!

Vocal Directed by GDLO (MonoTree) Background Vocals by 조형원 / Dewain Whitmore / Patrick "J Que" Smith Recorded by 권유진, 민성수 @ doobdoob Studio / GDLO @ MonoTree Studio Pro Tools Operating by GDLO (MonoTree) Digital Editing by GDLO @ MonoTree Studio / 노민지 @ SM SSAM Studio Engineered for Mix by 노민지 @ SM SSAM Studio Mixed by 정의석 @ SM Blue Cup Studio

Original Title: Sit Down! Original Writers: Harvey Mason Jr. / Kevin Randolph / Patrick "J Que" Smith / Dewain Whitmore / Brittany Marie Burton (aka. Britt Burton) Original Publishers: Harvey Mason Music Publishing LLC / EKKO Music Rights (powered by CTGA) / Hundredup East (ASCAP) / Buddy & Bear Publishing (SESAC) / Avex Music Publishing Inc. / Seven Peaks Music (ASCAP) a/b/o Itself and 8Sixteen Music (ASCAP) / BMB Top Songs / WC Music Corp. Sub-Publishers: EKKO Music Rights (powered by CTGA) / Universal Music Publishing Korea / Warner Chappell Music Korea Inc.

메아리(LOVE ME NOW)

짙은 이 밤의 끝 점점 더 희미해져 멀어져 가 / 이제야 깨달아 빛났던 그때를 / 네가 사라진 어둠에 갇혀 홀로 남겨진 날들

끊임없이 울려 내 맘엔 널 향한 소리 번진 메아리 / yeah 흐린 시간 너머 손을 뻗어 품 안에 널 안을래

*oh but I know 이미 한참 늦어버린 나란 걸 / 너의 숨소리 내 주위를 맴도는 걸 / 이 밤 가득 밀려오는 메아리 / 이제 난 목놓아 계속 널 부르는 이 순간

**I want you to love me now (I want you to love me now) / I want you to love me now (I want you to love me now) / I want you to love me now yeah yeah yeah / 널 외치고 불러 love me now come love me now oh

***터질 듯한 심장이 love me love me love me / 쏟아낸 이 메아리 love me love me love me / baby love me love me now / 다시 love me love me now yeah

yeah 겁이 나 네가 자꾸 생각나 / 길을 걷다 우연히 네 향기가 난 또다시 너를 찾아 / 비가 내려와 그대로 데려가 / 너와 입을 맞추던 길 이제는 둘 아닌 홀로 yeah yeah

몰아쉬는 깊은 한숨에 점점 짙어진 널 향한 울림 / 잠든 기억 너머 발을 디뎌 희미한 널 잡을래

*Repeat

**Repeat

***Repeat

어느새 내 맘이 너에게도 전해지길 네가 듣게 / 나를 봐줘 그때의 너처럼 please come love me once again

oh girl I know 우린 차마 돌이킬 수 없어도 / 서로의 거린 좁혀지기 힘들어도

하염없이 돌고 도는 너란 꿈 / 그 소릴 따라 너를 찾아가 지금처럼

**Repeat

***Repeat

love me love me love me / love me love me love me

love me love me love me / 다시 love me love me now yeah

Korean Lyrics by
Le'mon (153/Joombas) /
Rick Bridges (X&)

Composed by
Mike Daley /
Mitchell Owens / DEEZ /
Wilbart "Vedo" McCoy III

Arranged by
Mike Daley /
Mitchell Owens

Vocal Directed by DEEZ Background Vocals by Andrew Choi / Wilbart "Vedo" McCoy III Recorded by 권유진, 민성수 @ doobdoob Studio / 김완민 @ 게니리싸운드 Digital Editing by 이지홍 @ SM LVYIN Studio Engineered for Mix by 이지홍 @ SM LVYIN Studio Mixed by 이지홍 @ SM LVYIN Studio

Original Title: Love Me Now Original Writers: Mike Daley / Mitchell Owens / DEEZ / Wilbart "Vedo" McCoy III Original Publishers: Ritchie Court (ASCAP) / EKKO Music Rights (powered by CTGA)

우산 (Love song)

Korean Lyrics by
서지음 / 태용 / 마크 / 쟈니

Composed by
Jonathan Yip /
Ray Romulus /
Jeremy Reeves /
Ray McCullough / DEEZ /
Bianca "Blush" Atterberry

Arranged by
The Stereotypes / DEEZ

너를 향해 기운 우산이 이렇게 때마침 참 작아서 다행이야 / hoo 이런 건 예상하지 못한 상황이야 어깨가 닿은 이 순간

'어디 들어갈 델 찾자' 말하면서도 내 걸음은 / 자꾸만 하염없이 느려져 I can't stop I can't stop this feeling

너의 숨소리도 들려 이렇게 가까우니까 / 이대로 투명해진 채 시간이 멈췄으면 해 yeah

*비는 질색인데 오늘 좀 좋아지려 해 / 아니 아직 그칠 생각은 말고 왼쪽 어깨는 흠뻑 적셔 놔도 돼 / 빗속의 Love song Love song Love song yeah 둘만의 섬을 만들어 ooh / 이렇게 Love this Love this Love this rain 떨어지는 빗속에 all day

오늘따라 더 익숙한 거리도 헤매고 싶어 난 / ooh '저번 그 예쁜 카페가 어디더라' 잘 기억나지 않아

너의 눈에 내가 비쳐 이렇게 가까우니까 / 날 보며 웃음 지을 땐 심장이 멎을 것 같아 yeah

*Repeat

in this place just you and me / outside all blurry my focus clear as day 2.0 2.0 / warm and cozy covering us from all the crazy

rain don't stop 비 내려와 둘이서 1인용 umbrella 아래 / 내 하루는 so bright 떠올라 넌 지지 않는 나의 빛

doo-doo-doo- rain drop hop out my foreign car / 흠뻑 젖은 이 아스팔트 위에는 한편의 scene을 만들어내지

어느새 여기 내 안에 네가 겹쳐와 / 내 맘속에 너는 저 촉촉한 비처럼 / 스며들어와

*Repeat

Vocal Directed by DEEZ Background Vocals by Andrew Choi / Bianca "Blush" Atterberry Recorded by 권유진, 민성수 @ doobdoob Studio
Digital Editing by 노민지 @ SM SSAM Studio Engineered for Mix by 노민지 @ SM SSAM Studio Mixed by 김한구 @ sound POOL studios

Original Title: Luv Song Original Writers: Jeremy Reeves / Jonathan Yip / Ray Romulus / Ray McCullough / DEEZ / Bianca "Blush"
Atterberry Original Publishers: Sumphu / WC Music Corp. / Music For Milo / Warner-Tamerlane Publishing Corp. / Please Enjoy The
Music / Sony/ATV Songs LLC / Charm N Hammer Music / Sounds By The Beach / EKKO Music Rights (powered by CTGA) / Seven
Summits Music (BMI) o/b/o Itself and High Rise Life Publishing Sub-Publishers: Warner Chappell Music Korea Inc. / Sony/ATV Music
Publishing Korea

백야:(White Night)

조용히 어두워지고 금방 비가 올 듯해 여전히 먹먹한 이런 날씨가 너는 좋은지 / '잘 지내?' 묻지 못해 난 왜 잊지 못하고 낮과 밤이 온통 너인데 ooh

아직도 난 이렇게 지내 알잖아 조금 이해해줘 날 / 오늘도 난 여기서 또 잠 못 든 채 너를 잊어가

*혼자만의 긴 안녕 (better eatin' nice sleepin' don't know what it is) / 잠 못 드는 오늘도 all night long / 참 길어져 버린 이별에 우습게 보일 나지만 인사를 건네 안녕

(ooh) 오늘도 오늘도 all night long / (ooh) yeah

차라리 이 모든 게 다 꿈이라면 좋겠어 / 난 이미 꿈보다 꿈같은 곳에 살아

your face your skin your voice / (네 모든 건) 지울 수가 없을까 / 자꾸만 더 (자꾸 더 점점 더) / 선명해져 가 ooh

아직도 난 이렇게 지내 잠들지 못한 기억을 혼자 / 걷다가 널 찾다가 또 뜬 눈으로 밤을 새우지

*Repeat

억지로 잠을 청해보다 스친 꿈에도 너를 만나 / 전부 너란 시간 속에 오늘도

새하얀 밤 (better eatin' nice sleepin' don't know what it is) / oh 너를 그려 all night long (all night long night long) / 내쉬는 숨 (숨을 내쉬면 익숙한 목소리) / 네 목소리 들려와 난 아직 (들려 난 아직) / 너를 꿈꾸다 all night long

(ooh) ya 나의 꿈 나의 꿈은 아직 너야 yeah yeah / (ooh) 이 밤 all night all night long / (ooh) 너를 너를 너를 그리는 그리는 이 밤 / (ooh) 안녕 all night long all night long

Korean Lyrics by
지유리 (JamFactory) / JQ / 혜수 (makeumine works)

Composed by
Kenzie / Harvey Mason Jr. / Kevin Randolph / Dewain Whitmore / Ester Na / Sadie Currey

Arranged by
Harvey Mason Jr. / Kevin Randolph

Vocal Directed by DEEZ Background Vocals by NCT 도영 Recorded by 권유진, 민성수 @ doobdoob Studio Digital Editing by 노민지 @ SM SSAM Studio Engineered for Mix by 노민지 @ SM SSAM Studio Mixed by 김철순 @ SM Blue Ocean Studio

Original Title: Feels Like Love Original Writers: Kenzie / Harvey Mason Jr. / Kevin Randolph / Ester Na / Sadie Currey / Dewain Whitmore Original Publishers: EKKO Music Rights (powered by CTGA) / Harvey Mason Music Publishing LLC / Hundredup East (ASCAP) / Hundredup West (BMI) / Seven Peaks Music (ASCAP) o/b/o Itself and 8Sixteen Music (ASCAP) Sub-Publishers: EKKO Music Rights (powered by CTGA) / Universal Music Publishing Korea

NOT Alone

Korean Lyrics by
조윤경

Composed by
Nicki Adamsson /
Michael Matosic /
Michelle Elaine Buzz

Arranged by
Nicki Adamsson

매일 같은 꿈을 꿔 정답을 모른 채 나를 막아선 많은 것들에 무뎌져야 해 / 누군가를 만나고 때론 멀어지곤 해 때로는 버겁고 또 막연한 듯해 불안해질 때

써 내려 가 담담히 하루 하루 하루 지나는 사이 견뎌야 하는 많은 것들 / 지친 발 걸음을 적신 외로움은 말이 없네 그저 조용히

*한 걸음씩 한 걸음씩 한 걸음씩 / 가까워진 가까워진 가까워진 / 나를 닮은 꿈에 비친 그곳으로 Can you feel not alone? baby / 변함없이 변함없이 변함없이 / 이어지길 이어지길 이어지길 / 함께 걷는 함께 걷는 이 길에선 We are never alone

매일 같은 꿈을 꿔 이유도 모른 채 눈이 부신 걸 난 따라가야 해 oh 걸어가야 해 (숨 가빠도) / 언젠가 기나긴 이 길을 지나온 가슴이 떨리게 rebound 눈앞에 eh eh (eh eh)

모든 게 so I love it 까만 밤이 / 더 길어진 대도 두렵지 않아 내 꿈을 더 끌어안아

본 것 같아 간절한 모든 모든 모든 꿈들이 다 이뤄진 시간 속에 문득 / 마주친 너의 그 눈빛에 날 담아 떠오르던 지난 시간이

*Repeat

눈을 감아 맘을 담아 / 너를 부르면 곧 느껴지는 걸

so just

*Repeat

Vocal Directed by 서미래 (ButterFly) Background Vocals by NCT 도영 / 주찬양 (ICONIC SOUNDS) Recorded by 노민지 @ SM Yellow Tail Studio / 권유진, 인성수 @ doobdoob Studio / 정호진 @ sound POOL studios / 이민규 @ SM Big Shot Studio / 김광민 @ 개나리싸운드 Pro Tools Operating by 서미래 (ButterFly) Digital Editing by 서미래 (ButterFly) / 이민규 @ SM Big Shot Studio / 노민지 @ SM SSAM Studio Engineered for Mix by 이민규 @ SM Big Shot Studio / 노민지 @ SM SSAM Studio Mixed by 남궁진 @ SM Concert Hall Studio

Original Title: Feel It Alone Original Writers: Nicki Adamsson / Michael Matosic / Michelle Elaine Buzz Original Publishers: Publishing Company TEN, admin by Kobalt Music Publishing, Ltd. / Kobalt Music Publishing Ltd (KMP) obo Hillside Sounds Inc / Matosic Music / Buzz Recordings / WC Music Corp. Sub-Publishers: Music Cube, Inc. / Warner Chappell Music Korea Inc.

credits

Executive Producer
SM ENTERTAINMENT Co., Ltd.

Producer
SOO-MAN LEE

Music & Sound Supervisor
유영진

Producing Director
이성수

A&R Direction & Coordination
채정희, 허민영, 고아라, 김혜원

International A&R
이진현, 김동구, 이정민, 오세융, 이종원

Choreography Direction
홍성용, 염희섭

Choreographers
[영웅 (英雄: Kick It)]
Julian De Guzman,
The Quick Style, Brian Puspos, 정구성
[Punch]
Quick Style, Rie Hata,
Keone Madrid, Jinwoo Yoon

Music Licensing
오정은, 김민정

Music Production Management
유아름, 박민정, 위주미

Recorded by
YOO, YOUNG JIN
@ SM BOOMINGSYSTEM
정의석 @ SM Blue Cup Studio
이민규 @ SM Big Shot Studio
이지홍, 김은지 @ SM LVYIN Studio
노민지 @ SM Yellow Tail Studio
장우영, 권유진, 인성수 @ doobdoob Studio
GDLO @ MonoTree Studio
정호진 @ sound POOL studios
김광민, 홍수연 @ 개나리싸운드
정기홈 (assist. 최다인, 이찬미) @ Seoul
Studio

Mixed by
남궁진 @ SM Concert Hall Studio
김철순 @ SM Blue Ocean Studio
정의석 @ SM Blue Cup Studio
이민규 @ SM Big Shot Studio
이지홍 @ SM LVYIN Studio
김한구 @ sound POOL studios
구종필 @ KLANG STUDIO

Mastered by
권남우 @ 821 Sound Mastering

Management Director
탁영준

Artist Management & Promotion
강병준, 이승환, 임종범, 황진, 이중섭, 이성근

Artist Planning & Development
윤희준, 조유은, 신평화

Public Relations & Publicity
김지원, 정상희, 이자선, 임현정

Media Planning
김민성, 복민권, 허재혁, 김후식, 김인환

International Management & Promotion
최정민, 김현선

Music Distribution & Marketing
안수욱, 조동초, 유은정, 이가영, 정다은, 김다희,
김지원, 이상형

Customer Relationship Management
김지원, 탁윤주, 양효실

[SM USA]
Managing & Marketing Director
Dom Rodriguez, Jeremy Lopez

A&R Direction & Coordination
Janie Yoo, Victor Portillo, Steven M. Lee,
Mindy Somin Song

Artist Content Director
이상민

Music Video Direction & Arrangement
이상민, 김기현, 정민서

Music Video Director
GDW (Punch)

Track Video Director
이호수(cpbeq) (NonStop, 너의 하루)

Promotion Video Director
뭉하(wwhh)

Promotion Content Planning & Production
신다정, 정은비, 최수임, 허재윤, 박수현

SNS Content Planning & Management
신다정, 정은비

Graphic Design
이소희, 라혜수

Visual Planning
김소연

Photography
박종하

Video Sketch Photography
이씨헐, 김혜수

Set Styling
이서경(dadaobjet)

Styling
김영진

Hair Styling
한송희

Make-up
안성은

Executive Advisor
YOUNG-MIN KIM, SO-YOUNG NAM

Executive Supervisor
이성수, 탁영준

[Official Website]
nct127.smtown.com

[NCT Contents Lab]
www.nct2020.com

[Youtube Channel]
www.youtube.com/chnct
www.youtube.cowm/nct127
www.youtube.com/smtown

[Social Network Service]
Twitter www.twitter.com/NCTsmtown_127
Instagram www.instagram.com/nct127
Facebook www.facebook.com/NCT127.smtown
Weibo www.weibo.com/NCT127smtown

Dreams Come T...